Swap it!

Swap it!

Herein lie the secrets
that will help you
get rid of what
you never really wanted
and swap it for
something much better

ANDREW SERCOMBE

Guildford, Surrey

Copyright © 2001 Andrew Sercombe

The right of Andrew Sercombe to be identified as author of this work has been asserted by him in accordance with the Copyright, Designs and Patents Act 1988.

British Library Cataloguing in Publication Data. A catalogue record for this book is available from the British Library.

Published by Eagle Publishing Ltd, PO Box 530, Guildford, Surrey GU2 4FH.

Illustrations © 2001 Tim Charnick

All rights reserved. No part of this publication may be reproduced or transmitted in any form or by any means, electronic or mechanical, including photocopying, recording or any information storage and retrieval system, without either prior permission in writing from the publisher or a licence permitting restricted copying. In the United Kingdom such licences are issued by the Publishers Licensing Society Ltd, 90 Tottenham Court Road, London W1P 9HE.

Typeset by Eagle Publishing
Printed by Cox & Wyman, Reading
ISBN No: 0 86347 450 0

Contents

	Introduction	7
1.	It's Like This ...	9
2.	Mr Moore	13
3.	The Swap Shop	17
4.	My Rule Book	19
5.	'What Do You Want Instead?'	24
6.	Josh	27
7.	How Rebecca Became a Lion	29
8.	Grown UP – or Grown DOWN?	34
9.	Living in a Bubble?	39
10.	You're in Control!	46
11.	On the Inside	48
12.	Raw Reality	50
13.	Have Some Fun with your Brain!	56
14.	Little Boxes	60
15.	The Swap of a Lifetime	66
16.	Letting Go	72
17.	OK, so who is 'Plenty Moore'?	77
18.	Experiment ...	78

Introduction

Swap it! is about letting go of something you don't want and swapping it for something better. Thousands, millions of people just like you and me would dearly love to find a way to get rid of what they have right now and simply swap it for something else, something better.

As a Powerchange Life Coach I have learnt all sorts of interesting, and more importantly, *effective* ways for people to achieve that swap. Ordinary people across the world are living better lives and enjoying them much more because they allowed their lives to progress: they let go of what they were gripping tightly onto and swapped it for something better.

Quite frequently, in fact more often than not, they were swapping to something ini-

Swap it!

tially unfamiliar, a bit strange. The new ways, whilst being so much more comfortable and down to earth, not to mention much more fun, were just that – new. Just like moving to a new house, it took a bit of getting used to. However, it was a delight to get used to it! Who wants old, sadly lacking ways of thinking and being, especially when they seem to hurt or be uncomfortable, when you can have ways of thinking and being that REALLY work, that are comfortable and satisfying deep down.

1. It's Like This . . .

To illustrate what might happen to your life as you read this book, and how much better it can be to live differently, I want to tell you about a woman I knew as Petra who had a very un-relaxing home in Eastern Europe. Petra was moved into an apartment that was shocking in more ways than one. Her central heating radiators had been wrongly connected and gave electric shocks to whichever unsuspecting visitor touched them. And the lights in her home refused to work, so she used oil lamps, which she lit every evening as the daylight faded.

Unable to do anything about these two problems and unaware that they might be linked, she moved her furniture around her home so that people were less likely to touch the radiators by accident. Petra lived for years like this, and got quite used to it.

Swap it!

It was only when someone visited that she would remember something was wrong.

One day, in the late afternoon as the sun was setting on the horizon, Petra had a visitor. She had heard about him from a friend who lived in the same block and had asked to see him; he was a smart electrician. Petra explained her situation and the electrician smiled. He went to a box on the wall, took a screwdriver from his back pocket and simply swapped ONE WIRE from one place to another. It took three minutes. Smiling, he asked Petra to try the lights. They worked perfectly. 'Touch the radiators,' the electrician suggested. Petra had long since decided this was not a good idea, but the man reassured her, 'They won't hurt you now.'

On the basis of that reassurance she overcame her fears for a moment and cautiously reached out her hand . . .

Never had Petra been so pleased to feel nothing! Was this real? Was the central heating system finally safe?

The following days and weeks were very interesting for Petra. It took her a while to work out the best places for her furniture. Some of it was thrown out or sold (she'd got hold of several protective items over the years that she wouldn't be needing any more) and her other things were placed around her home where she really wanted them. They would be employed much more usefully doing what they were designed for.

The electrician had joked that if she wanted it all back again it would be very easy to do, but it couldn't happen accidentally. No way, she thought to herself! Although for a few weeks it was likely to be a bit strange,

Swap it!

she could handle that! It was SO MUCH BETTER LIKE THIS.

As you read this book I suspect *you will remember* the things you want to swap for something better. Make a list as you go. This book will give you some simple skills you can acquire in order to live much freer than you have in the past, even though, like Petra, you or your friends may have thought that electric shocks from *your* 'personal heating system' was quite normal.

2. Mr Moore

Not far away and well within walking distance, is an amazing little shop. On the outside it looks like any other shop, stuck in the middle of a short terrace with bright, attractive and well-kept little boutiques thriving on each side. It has a clean, neat frontage, a tidy door, brightly painted in your favourite colour, and an old wooden counter. It has the smell of a quality antique shop – that sort of beeswaxy, musty, oil-painty smell, with a hint of old books. The shop exudes a feeling of *joie de vivre*, typified by the friendly chattering and laughter that provides the reassuring background atmosphere. As you approach it, note the tingling sensation of gentle excitement you feel, see if you can try and resist the joyful anticipation welling up within you. This is clearly a different sort of shop. It is blatantly IRRESISTIBLE. And once you discover its charms you have no inten-

Swap it!

tion of resisting it anyway!

Inside, it is literally a world away from the average high street boutique. The small innocent frontage belies its cavernous interior. The shop is a delectable rabbit warren of interesting corridors and storerooms. It is gorgeous and the man who runs it does nothing but add to its attraction. He is both wise and clever – a rare combination. It is thought that the proprietor has several degrees from the most ancient of universities, but that is only hearsay. You could never tell, for he speaks just like the ordinary man in the street with no funny accent or peculiar mannerisms. He's – well, just nice. Sort of approachable. Understanding. Easy to be with. And . . . *wise*.

His name. Oh, yes. His name is Moore. Mr Moore. And his nickname? 'Plenty.'

Of course Plenty isn't his real name. No one can remember what that is and he never tells. He is old, yet has none of that 'oldness' that you can see on the faces of other people perhaps thirty years his junior. Mr Moore lives alone over the shop and appears to be compulsively happy, despite occasional illness. One very interesting thing about Mr Moore is that he is so open and honest, not in a vulnerable way, but sort of 'reassuringly' honest – a bit like when people joke about an item being 'reassuringly expensive'. He is generous to a fault, which probably accounts for his nickname. Apart from those attributes, Plenty Moore has never been heard to speak badly of others (ever) and has an unnerving lack of pride. He has just one pet hate: being called Old Moore. It's not wise to call him that.

Sadly, though, Plenty Moore does have a

Swap it!

few enemies. It is amazing how so many nice people do, isn't it? It is almost as if somehow their niceness is a threat. Actually, Mr Moore *can* appear threatening if you want to try to persuade him to do something unethical or damaging. He sets that 'look' of his that makes you realise that the comment is beneath you and then you wish (like crazy!) that the thought had not even entered your head.

Oh, yes. One other thing about Mr Moore: when you are with him it feels as if he knows what you're thinking without you telling him. Now that *is* a bit scary.

3. The Swap Shop

And the shop Mr Moore runs? It's *The Swap Shop*. His vast emporium is filled with better things than the ones you and I have – mostly anyway. Mr Moore does everything possible to see that his clients go out of his shop with something better than what they came in with. His 'exchange values' are unbelievable, and the shop is a Cash Free Zone. He simply won't take money – cash, cheques, credit cards – anything – as part of a deal. Refuses point blank. You just 'owe it to him', knowing that he rarely collects. (There's been a lot of local speculation on that one. What do *you* think?)

In fact, rumours abound about the Swap Shop. And jokes too. Many a person struggling with something they know is not ideal, or is hurtful, or that they don't want

Swap it!

to happen, are all too likely to receive the witty comment, 'There's always Moore!' And the humour is well placed. Perhaps a few hours later the struggling party can be seen making her way, as discreetly as possible, down towards the little terrace of boutiques, to return with something most definitely better.

4. My Rule Book

I took my rule book to Mr Moore. I've never seen it since.

I was brought up with a rule book. It wasn't a written one, but a rule book in my head. It told me that there was just one right way to do things and many wrong ways, and it was all too easy to do things one of the large number of wrong ways, while to find the right way was a tough, difficult and up-hill task. The rule book was sort of hidden around the corner most of the time and kept getting moved to a new secret location without me noticing. Sometimes it was blatantly obvious, on a shelf high up where everyone could see it, and high enough to be frustratingly beyond reach. At other times I never quite knew where it would turn up next.

I was brought up within a deeply religious

environment, as my parents had been before me. We knew what rules were all about. We were expected to do things *right* – whatever that was.

Now there was one snag in all this. Different people had different views on what the 'right' way was. So 'right' was not always immediately obvious – which can be a little unnerving when you are a divergent, creative and sensitive thinker like myself. And the brand of religion to which I belonged seemed to attract some very authoritarian and dominating people. Looking back, I lived with a subtle and undermining fear of getting it wrong – all too easy when there were so many ways available. I struggled with self-confidence, and because of that lack, I needed others to make up for its absence. I fed on approval. That is not a particularly healthy way to live.

The rule book in my head was very clear on lots of things. If I obeyed the rules I would be accepted and acceptable. If I disobeyed ... well, a special sort of guilt was heading in my direction by the truckload, and it usually hit just before bedtime. It isn't always so easy to sleep through the night with a truckload of guilt in your brain.

In the first eight or ten years of my life it didn't matter too much. A sense of loving discipline and security pervaded our family home, and my wonderful parents provided an atmosphere of acceptance and care. It was from my teenage years on that the cracks began to show. My sensitive, freedom-seeking spirit was coming alive. The methods of an old, controlling, legalistic religion began to be exposed. I had been living by an imposed set of what I discovered were phoney rules – rules that didn't really work and weren't always true. Rules that controlled me.

Swap it!

How long would it take before I discovered that rules are intended to free and enable, to provide a framework for the future, a sort of flexing and mobile skeleton inside?

Eventually I discovered that I was not designed to live, or die, in any sort of strait-jacket – even an invisible one – and especially not by the mother of all rule books that resided half way between my ears.

I took the rule book to the Swap Shop. I wanted to talk to Mr Moore about it. I just had to get rid of it. If I had kept it much longer I would have had a nervous breakdown. Heaving it onto the counter was a watershed in my life. Mr Moore heard the crash and came out into the shop from his office.

'So you want to get rid of that do you?'

Did I!

'What do you want instead?'

Swap it!

5. 'What Do You Want Instead?'

Do you know, until that moment I had never really thought about that. I had got used to obeying the rules and doing the Right Thing however uncomfortable or demanding it was. And here I was with the possibility of a choice. I took on Plenty Moore's question and asked it of myself:

What DO you want instead?

Mr Moore invited me round into one of his cavernous rooms at the back of his shop. Steering me to the appropriate section, he said that this section was getting increasingly popular as lots of people were now coming to the Swap Shop with their rule books. Some of these rule books people carried had come from a very strict parent (whose parent had had it before that, and passed it down). Others had acquired theirs from school teachers, some from the army. Occasionally a customer had written the rule book themselves when they were younger in order to make themselves feel better. You did feel better if you kept all your own rules. Mr Moore had issued all sorts of alternatives, but not to worry because, yes, you've guessed it, there were 'plenty more'.

He offered me a rather petite suspicious looking (to the uninitiated eye) book, creatively decorated with the four points of the compass. He explained that it was a little collection of stories from around the world bound into a unique Guide Book. I was amazed to find my name was already written on the flyleaf. (How did he know?!) I would be wise to keep it close to hand, he said, so that I could consult it. There was a story for most of the situations I'd find

Swap it!

myself in and I could read one when I was stuck. It had a little section that held a map, another that held a compass and, as I turned the pages over the years I would learn Guiding Principles that would enable me to live free, without becoming wild. Like a horse that had been 'broken in' I would be able to use all my creativity, strength and freedom, but purposefully and with skill.

I wanted to hug 'Plenty' as I left. The thought of living the way he suggested was so exciting. I knew life would never be the same again.

And it hasn't been.

6. Josh

One of the people my new freedom helped me to understand was Josh.

Josh was a twelve-year-old boy in my Technology class and I was his teacher. He was a non-conformist by nature. He thought differently to the others in his class. He saw different things, approached problems and tasks with his own unique style and struggled to do his work the 'right' way. I suspect he would echo the D.H. Lawrence character who said, 'My life won't go down the proper channels – it just won't.' And inevitably Josh got into trouble. He was rarely deliberately naughty, it was just that he seemed to march to the beat of a different drum. He kept finding himself out of step, bored, late to lessons, unwittingly messing things up.

Swap it!

Josh and I got on so well because I showed him how he could be free from the rule book – at least in my lessons. And was it worth it! He now worked harder than anyone else, drew and wrote far more than he had done before, to a higher standard, and finished a brilliant project. His project didn't look like anyone else's of course. Nor did it function like anyone else's. But it was great – colourful, interesting, thought out and full of special unexpected additions. He'd worked at that project day and night! His was the envy of the class.

Josh learnt a lot more than technology in my lessons. He learnt about living free and thinking free.

7. How Rebecca Became a Lion

And what about Rebecca? Rebecca is a very intelligent girl of eighteen. We sat over a cup of machine coffee in a leisure centre for our coaching appointment. If Rebecca had been in the Swap Shop with Mr Moore she would have had *lots* of things on the counter – and one of them would probably have been a mouse! Not an actual mouse, though. Rebecca had the impression that she WAS a 'mouse', deep inside herself. Mice are not very highly respected, and are easily trodden on and trapped. That was Rebecca! In fact she had got so used to it she would tread on *herself*! So we had to do something about that. The conversation went something like this:

Rebecca, what animal do you admire for its courage?

Swap it!

> *A lion!*
> *I want you to imagine a lion over there, about two metres away! Can you see it?*
> *Yes. (Isn't imagination a wonderful thing!)*
> *Describe it to me.*
> *It is a friendly lion, but very strong and powerful. It is afraid of nothing and nobody. It likes me!*

We stood up from the table and looked at the lion together. It certainly was a powerful and fearless beast. (I was getting quite nervous myself!)

> *Let it come closer, Rebecca. Closer! Closer still! Give that lion permission to come right inside you and look through your eyes! Let it give you the strength and courage it has. What do you think the lion is thinking now?*

The change in Rebecca's posture was dra-

Rebecca found that practising her new skill produced some interesting reactions.

Swap it!

matic and her attitude completely altered. She stood up straight and tall (she had been hunched and timid) and a fearlessness appeared in her face. Rebecca was enjoying this. In fact we were both trying very hard not to laugh.

As Rebecca stood there with the 'lion' deep down inside her, she knew she could and would be different from here on. We played around with the lion, it went back to the other part of the room, then 'into' her again. Every time she did this the confidence and strength she was searching for returned to her face and physique. Every time she felt bold and invincible. What a transformation!

We discussed the options:

> When **you can have a lion**, you are going to hate mousedom!

Yes!
*If you can have lion qualities for five minutes, how would it be for you to know **they are there forever?***

Well, her reaction was pretty much the same as yours.

Mr Moore would have been proud of me. In fact I think he probably is.

By the way, take as much time as **you** need to decide to play with your own lion. Don't rush the decision. Learning to play 'Lion' may just mean you have more courage, strength, cleverness and determination than you ever dreamed ...

And what will that *be* like?

Let me know as soon as possible.

Swap it!

8. Grown UP – or Grown DOWN?

Being grown up can have some MAJOR disadvantages! One reason is we forget how to be like little children again. You know – simple, curious, trusting, fun-loving. That sort of little child.

The last few years for me have been a voyage of discovery BACKWARDS. Growing DOWN time.

So it was another trip to the Swap Shop. This time it was much easier, because I didn't have to take anything but myself. As I walked in, the little doorbell tinkled its merry tune and as if by magic Mr Moore appeared.

'Can I help you?'

'Yes.' And I climbed up onto the counter!

Plenty Moore smiled his gentle wise smile. He'd been here before and seemed to know what was coming. Polite as ever, he asked me to explain. (He knew I needed to tell him.)

'I'm fed up with constantly being so adult,' I told him. 'I want to be free to be like a little child again. However,' I continued quickly, 'I will still need to be an adult a lot of the time!'

'That's fine!' he told me. 'Both are equally important. What you really need is to be able to swap them over at will. You need a sort of mobile Swap Shop you can take with you and use as you want to.'

'Is that possible?' I asked incredulously, imagining what it would be like to cart his

Giles the butler experienced just the slightest tingle of excitement as he remembered again the taste of fizzy-pop.

shop around with me!

'Oh, yes. All things are possible to those who believe!' He'd used this line somewhere else and was grinning from ear to ear.

So that was it. He suggested that I took the mobile Swap Shop home in my head and practised with it a good few times so that I knew what I was doing and would be able to get really skilled with it. He showed me how to play at being child-like – 'not child-*ish*' – and then quickly swap back to being adult when that was more appropriate.

I can't begin to tell you how much fun it was – and still is. I let a few of my friends in on the secret and the more sophisticated ones thought I was a bit odd. Several said they envied me. One or two quietly remarked, 'It's great, isn't it!' in a secretive

Swap it!

sort of way. (They were the ones I'd always felt were the most normal too.)

And to think I never knew!

9. Living in a Bubble?

Plenty Moore has become a very good friend to me. I have learnt to trust him implicitly. He is everything you could wish for in a friend. And it is a pleasure to share his friendship with his other customers and clients – and those who pop into the Swap Shop just for a chat and his amazing pearls of wisdom. Every now and then he takes me on one side and lets me in on one or two of his tricks. Skills, he calls them. *Living in the Bubble* is one of his favourites for helping clients enjoy life extravagantly. Here it is for you just as he told it to me and, luckily, you can do it anywhere.

Like most of his techniques you'll need your imagination turned up!

Into the bubble . . .
1. **Imagine** you are holding your life like a

Swap it!

fine transparent bubble in both your hands – a tiny little world in this big universe being held out in front of you right now. (When I did this 'my life' was about 10cm in diameter.)

2. As it doesn't seem very big like that, **grow it**. Bigger. Bigger. Bigger still. You will have to rest it on the floor right now as it will be about 2 metres in diameter. Inflate it to about 3 metres in diameter. You should be able to see right into it from the outside.

3. Here's the fun bit. **Step into the bubble**. Do it quite slowly and deliberately. You may even be able to imagine the transparent bubble of film press against your face as you push yourself forwards into the globe. Be aware of it closing behind you.

4. **Notice** how much of what was outside the bubble is now inside it, but very pres-

ent indeed. The colours in the bubble – are they brighter or duller? What about the things you can hear? Are they sharper and crisp or not so defined? Look around the bubble and you will notice it is different in here for you.

5. **Enjoy the experience!** Now imagine a gigantic instant inflation inside the bubble, right where you are. Rather than popping the bubble (it is far too tough for that) the gigantic inflation blows the bubble to such a size that it encompasses the farthest limits of the Earth – and maybe the universe too if your imagination can do that for you!

So here you are, reading this book inside the massively huge bubble of your life. What do you notice about your life right now? Interesting isn't it? This sense of being *very present* in your world leaves little experience of past or future. It is ALL NOW, as

Swap it!

if you are living within Time itself – to such an extent that you become aware of its absence.

And back again ...

As you are fully right where you are now, allow the bubble to shrink again. Watch as the transparent skin of the bubble slowly comes in from way out there and stops just beyond your touch. (Notice how if you move, walk or run in the bubble when it's like this it comes with you!)

Step out backwards, the way you came in, with the transparent film of the bubble sliding around you as you push yourself out through it, and closing to a perfect sphere in front of you now.

Step back a little from it and shrink it down to a size that you can now pick up in your hands – back to where you were before.

You can now put the sphere of your life down and stand back from it. You may be able to get it to hang in mid air in front of you so you can see it easily. You may want to see it in the context of the other things around it. Other people's spheres, for instance. Is it still or moving? If it is going to travel, what direction is your sphere going to take? Where are you heading? Is there a direction that may be more helpful for you and for the others around you?

Think about it. Perhaps a plan for the future might be helpful. Or perhaps you need to be less obsessive about the plan you stick to so rigidly and enjoy the moment some more from *inside* the bubble!

And in the other direction
You can stop there or you can do something new:

Swap it!

1. **Pick up the sphere** and hold it in your hands again.

2. Keep the transparent bubble of your life **shrinking to smaller and smaller**, until it is microscopically tiny and can slip between the cells of your skin to the inside of you!

3. Imagine it's inside now. You can give it permission to silently **grow to fill all of you from the inside.** If you grow it some more you can feel as if you are 'bursting' with life! Or you can have it any size you like. What works best for you?

4. And when you've had a play with that, **shrink it again**, pop it through the skin of your hand back into your palms. There it is!

What was that like for you?

I have little doubt that *something* happened.

See if you can identify what that is for you.

Try it again when you are in a different mood.

Swap it!

10. You're in Control!

It is good to have some control over how you experience your life isn't it? You may realise it's useful to be more 'in the bubble' sometimes. Or you may spend nearly all your time in there as it is, so stepping out of it for a while may be more helpful for you! Some situations will benefit from an engaged, In-the-Bubble approach. Others will serve you better if you are away from them a bit, Out-of-the-Bubble. Now you have a choice!

When Plenty Moore showed me this little skill, I realised I had lived long stretches of my life outside the bubble, as a sort of observer of my world. I determined to get a more enjoyable balance. It really has enhanced the pleasure I get from living each day. I slipped the skill into the mobile Swap Shop for everyday use and I play going in and out when I'm on journeys or waiting for someone! One real benefit of doing this is that you can experience yourself differently.

What are some of the more useful and enjoyable ways to keep that control?

I've shown you a few different ways you can operate. There are lots more you can discover.

Swap it!

11. On the Inside

I want to find out more about the Swap Shop. I want an inside perspective. All sorts of questions surfaced in my mind when I first discovered it and I'm asking even more now! How does Plenty Moore know? What other skills does he have? How can I have more of them too? How does he make his resources SO useful to other people? What does he feel like when people shun him and his wisdom? Perhaps I could run a Swap Shop too? (In fact, that's what I do these days!)

I know the answer to getting the answers! I am getting to know Plenty Moore better, and ask a lot of him. If he wants to keep things a secret that is up to him. I was not having him say to me in years to come, 'You didn't have the knowledge and understanding you wanted because you didn't ask me for it.' I've found he is only too delighted to answer the questions I have.

However, not everything goes quite as expected ...

12. Raw Reality

At this juncture you may want to point out that this is a story, and it would be very easy to mix up reality and my imagination.

Of course you're right.

However, I would like to ask you: How much of your past experience is reality right now? Do you have the *actual* past, or simply your *memories* of it? How do you know that what you've remembered about the past is accurate? And how accurate is it?

It was a huge relief to me when I realised that the past is something I *remember* and not something I *have*. It was a relief for two reasons:

1. I can change the way I remember it *without any loss of integrity*.

2. I can make those memories the way they will be most useful to my own future and the future of others.

I can bring my unhappy, uncomfortable memories to the 'Swap Shop counter' any time I like and change them. Most of the time I will simply change something *about* them to make them better.

Let me illustrate.

Have you ever watched a TV programme with the volume turned down? Or the colour control moved to black and white? Both of these make a lot of difference to how you experience the programme. After a demanding day it can be stressful to walk into your home and find a loud TV blaring away. By turning the volume down we can reduce the stress, and even sit down and enjoy the film with the family!

Swap it!

Merely changing the colour of a film shot to 'sepia' (that yellowy colour of old films) we are led to think this film is old. If there is a lot of blood and gore in the film, it becomes much less shocking to see the film in black and white.

In my Powerchange Coaching practice I work with all sorts of men and women who were violently treated when they were small and certainly do not want to think about it again. Yet it still hurts them; tears will come the instant they revisit the memory. The sensitivity level of that experience is too high for comfort. They feel vulnerable, and often simply blank it out.

However, blanking it out doesn't change it. In fact it makes it even HARDER to forget. It simply stops us from approaching it and taking the pain out of it. And it may not be something we *want* to blank out completely.

The children soon realised that turning *dad* to sepia was the better option.

Swap it!

The death of a close friend can be a very special memory, yet if the pain level is too high we cannot enjoy the richness of their friendship with us without it hurting unbearably. So we 'don't go there'. How much better it would be to have the memory of their life as a special treasure that we can enjoy whenever we want, their death being an enriching aspect and not a torturous pain. You can trust your brain to go for the most pleasant (or least unpleasant) memory if it has a choice. So we give it some choices:

- Design your own sound track for that event.
- Change the background to something much more attractive.
- Put some loving and kind people into the picture.
- Have them say what you would like them to say.

- You tell them what you need to tell them.

You will never remember that situation the same again. Just like Petra at the beginning of this book you can put it all back as it was. However, I suspect you will, also like Petra, *keep the new version* and even improve it.

> How do you <u>not</u> think about **Blue Bananas?**
>
> Try your hardest NOT to think about **blue bananas**.
>
> Come on, STOP IT!
> It isn't easy.
> Or is it?
>
> You will *instantly* stop thinking about blue bananas when you think instead about
>
> **PINK FURRY ELEPHANTS**
> Now change their colour to any colour you like . . .
> See? You can do it!

Swap it!

13. Have Some Fun With Your Brain!

Choose an experience from your memory bank that you would like to play with to see what's possible. Go for one that is less significant for you to start with. You could choose something very simple, even like cleaning your teeth. Here we go ...

1. Take a moment or two to relax and get into 'playful mode'!
2. Imagine cleaning your teeth. Now 'flavour' the brush with your most favourite taste and 'clean your teeth' with it!
3. How's that?
4. Try it for a few seconds with the taste of a raw lemon on your imaginary brush and see what happens ... then revert to the much nicer one! Phew, that's better!
5. Your body will respond to this experi-

ment with your mouth watering, or perhaps puckering with the *thought* of the different flavours you're trying.
6. Try cleaning your teeth with an imaginary 'totally flavourless' toothpaste. How different was that?
7. Maybe you would like to link a brilliant memory of a *really nice experience* to the thought of *picking up* your toothbrush. What might that be like! (You'll never forget to clean your teeth again!)

That same method can alter the way you remember past experiences. And you can change ANYTHING about the way you remember it. Enjoy the possibilities.

Swap it!

> ### Instant Holiday
>
> David has revolutionised his visits to the dental surgery by using his creative skills like this:
> He lies back as the dentist treats his teeth and whisks himself off to a beautiful, idyllic, sun-drenched beach, and adds in whatever delights he fancies – most of which he can't afford! No long air flight, no airport queues, no lost baggage, fantastic hotel room, plenty of spending money, favourite friends for company . . .
> He's reluctant to go home!

Dr Richardson had never had a patient quite like this before.

Swap it!

14. Little Boxes

At some time or other most people have been puzzled by how another person behaves. During my early life I assumed that most people thought like I did, and when I didn't understand their logic or the way they lived, I thought there must be something 'wrong' with them. As life went on, my view changed, and I learnt more about people, popping them neatly into little boxes of one kind or another, and sealing down the lid so that I could know quite definitively as much as possible about them and be in control of what I thought they did or said. 'After all,' I told myself, 'people never change.' I felt secure with that.

As I went into business I watched people being boxed by their companies, with all sorts of different criteria being used for making the boxes. Psychometric testing is used a lot today to bring insight to our lives, and there are all sorts of tests, each claiming to be more accurate, more useful more ... whatever! Of course psychometric tests are often very good – and they are especially so when we remember that the moment we stop writing or ticking the boxes the test is ever-so-slightly out of date.

People do change, and often quite a lot. In fact it is IMPOSSIBLE to be the same today as you were yesterday. Every little experience you have of life actually changes you somehow. Even TAKING a test changes you! In fact you may be someone for whom the THOUGHT of taking the test changes you! Because you lived yesterday, or did that test this morning, or even anticipated taking it, you *can no longer* be the same.

That we cannot remain the same is quite

Swap it!

obvious in your physical body. As a little child growing up you got physically stronger and fitter until you reach a peak of fitness. Then as you get older you will get weaker and less 'fit' for the tough but enjoyable business we call life. When that peak occurs in your life, and the age you handle it, rather depends on who you are. We are all different.

The same principle of constant development applies to the mental, emotional and spiritual aspects of your life. You are very wise to give yourself permission and space to be different each day. You may not be wildly different from the day before, but you will not be the same.

So how does all this fit into the Swap Shop?
As I observe Plenty Moore, the way he accepts people, their longings and aspira-

tions, I am impressed with the way he treats everyone. No one is boxed. No one has to defend their status or position. And this enables them to come with what they REALLY want to swap in the front of their minds, ready for his immediate attention. There is no need for them to beat about the bush, to chatter for ages before they can talk honestly. A nice thing about books like this is that you are reading alone, quietly allowing the story to affect you. There is no one to get at you, or tell you what they think of you. You can just read the book and let whatever wants to happen happen. Great isn't it? Just think: you've not been assessed or had to do a series of personality tests. You are who you are, and I for one am delighted you're reading my little book. As we come to the last section of it I want to remind you of some of the people and situations we've met:

Swap it!

There was Petra, so desperate to have an environment around her that didn't shock people. (Me, too!)

There was Josh with his unique creativity and way of thinking that didn't quite go down the normal channels (thankfully).

Rebecca came in there somewhere. She swapped her mouse-dom for some lion qualities like courage and strength.

Oh yes, and I told you about my rule book and how wonderful it was to get rid of it for good.

What about you?
If you were to bring something to Mr Moore's famous Swap Shop, what might it be?

And what will you want instead?

I've swapped all sorts of things.

- I swapped outrage for acceptance.
- I took along my insecurity and took home a deep sense of inner strength.
- I appeared at the Swap Shop door with a powerful longing to succeed and went home with the equally powerful knowledge that I couldn't fail.
- I asked Plenty Moore to take my fear of rejection (it had dogged me for years!) and he replaced it with a most rewarding confidence.
- I replaced my self-consciousness with a rich awareness of the importance of others and the future. (Who was it who said 'We would be a lot less concerned about what people thought of us if only we realised how little they do!')

One very useful swap was this one ...

Swap it!

15. The Swap of a Lifetime

Gradually I realised why I was born, and what my purpose was. It was a relief to discover that I really was important to the world ...

***Out**: pointless wandering*

***In**: a huge sense of purpose*

There is nothing in all the world, it seems to me, as wonderfully motivating as a sense of purpose. I like to ask the question 'Why was I born?' And, contrary to the opinions of some, that is not an unreasonable question to ask! Surely each of us on the earth who can think sufficiently succinctly to know we are so alive, in this unique way human beings are, can ask that question and arrive at some sort of satisfying answer. You can ask it now: 'Why was I born? Why am I alive? What is the purpose of my life?' The question cannot be answered satisfactorily merely from within ourselves. It teases out something more from each person who dares to try the question out. The very act of asking it can be a challenge, as if we have to overcome a deep fear that there may be no answer and we will end up on a wild goose chase to nowhere.

I've answered that question to my own satisfaction. You can too.

What about the glue?

A few days ago I was with a delightful Scotsman in his late thirties. He had got through two marriages and was struggling to know how to make decisions about his future. Brian is a very capable executive with a huge global company, and knows what decisions are about. So why was it so difficult for him?

Swap it!

As we discussed his situation it became clear to Brian that he had no personal *basis* for decision-making in his life. He needed some more reliable foundational building blocks. Up to now the choices he had made had brought short-term satisfaction. He had had a good life, but it wasn't producing the fulfilment he longed for. It was as if he was building his life on what appeared to be rock, but wasn't. He had all the components right (well almost) but was missing the glue that held them together. As I took him to the station after our appointment we discussed that 'glue'. He needed to know why he was on this earth, so he could co-operate fully with that deep sense of purpose and be free of all the doubt, hesitancy and questioning.

Truckloads
Down at the Swap Shop, Mr Moore is very used to this sort of thing. He's seen it all

before! His solution is something called 'faith'. It is an old-fashioned term (it's an old problem) and a very important one. He dishes out faith by the truckload – or as much as you can handle at any rate!

We all have faith to one degree or another. We put faith in people every day. I bet if you made a full list of people you've had to trust recently it would be metres long! For me that would include other drivers on the road (to stay on their side of it), all sorts of retailers (trusting that their goods are not dangerous to my health), the dentist, the newscaster on the radio (is he deliberately withholding information that I need?) and thousands of others. Having everyday faith is normal and essential to good health. What a mess we get into when we stop trusting. For me personally, I decided to trust every day of my life and future to God. (I'm a Christian.) I'm glad I did. My

Swap it!

own sense of purpose has become integrated with what I believe is his outline plan for me and the rest of the world. Such a trust has put my ambitions and longings into a different orbit. I decided it was worth taking a long-term view about where it would be wise to invest my faith for that ultimate future too!

Programming-in the destination

My son at present works for a highly reputable German car manufacturer, and inside his car is a satellite navigation system that works out where he is and how he can get to his destination. However, he must first program in his destination; he needs to know where he is going. And before he decides that he needs a purpose.

There is nothing so pointless as travelling without purpose. For some it is to get away from something they don't like or want. For others it is to get to where they DO want to go. For all of us, the deeper satisfaction comes when we know the purpose of the journey.

However, once my son has established the purpose of his journey, he has to trust the system. The very pleasant woman's voice instructs him, 'At the next junction, turn left.' And so he does. He has learnt that the equipment is very reliable and does its job well. He has faith in it, and for the most part it is well placed. He arrives where he wants to go.

Now what about you. What is your purpose? Don't shrink from the question. It will shape your entire future.

Swap it!

16. Letting Go

Mr Moore has to point out to his clients from time to time that he runs a SWAP shop. He reminds them that the one condition that they go away with something better is that they LEAVE BEHIND the item they are swapping. He knows this is important for their full enjoyment of what they take away from the shop. It is in *letting go* of what we have that frees us to take hold of something better! Part of the reason for this is that some things in our lives are incompatible.

- A self-centred materialistic attitude does not co-habit too well with a spirit of generosity.
- An open honest lifestyle does not fit with cheating on your partner.
- Being ruthless with people at work – whoever they are – will clash eventually

with being kind to yourself.
- Love and hate don't remain categorised. They won't stay in boxes: 'I'll love my wife but hate my father.' Sooner or later the one will affect the other.

This is where that sense of purpose we've just discussed really comes into its own. 'What am I hoping to achieve by loving my wife?' 'How does hating my father help me achieve my purpose?' If you want to enjoy the benefits of love then you will have to surrender the hate because they refuse to live together. Take it to the Swap Shop. If you want to love, you'll find Plenty Moore ready and available for you! He dishes out only good stuff. He has no intention of providing anything that may hurt you. His values and purpose are settled in his mind.

I used to handle strong criticism, or even the mildest criticism at one stage, very

Swap it!

badly. A few negative comments and I was launched down the slippery slope and heading towards the pit. It isn't nice down there. As I matured I realised that those comments, and my over-the-top reaction to them were crippling me. They were hurting my family too. Sometimes I would smart from a bitter word for days – I didn't want to, but I did. It took me years to realise that I was not trapped in this behaviour. I could do something about it. To start with I needed to separate the words of those people from their intention. I realised eventually that their intention was not always what I thought. People criticise others for all sorts of reasons.

Here are some:

- To help themselves feel better. Beheading others has the effect of making yourself feel taller.

- Because they don't understand what you did – or perhaps your motive for doing what you did.
- They think it is a clever thing to do.
- They are genuinely concerned that you may get hurt by continuing the way you are.

> Criticism is a cheap virtue. It implies that you could do better without having to prove it.

- Their view of the world does not allow for you doing what you did.

Whatever the reason, I now know that I am no longer dependent on other people's approval. I've let go (for the most part anyway) of the crippling need of people agreeing with me. I've a few very special friends who I've given access to the deeper parts of me.

It was more of a relief than I can describe!

Swap it!

A quick self-check:
Am I still dependent on others in a less than helpful way?

What would it be like if I swapped that dependence for the sure knowledge that I am just fine, that my opinions are valuable, and that because I know they are I don't have to force them on others?

They might enjoy that too.

17. OK, so who is 'Plenty Moore'?

At the beginning of this book I introduced you to the Swap Shop and its wise and clever owner, Plenty Moore. As you've read these chapters I hope you have had fun formulating in your mind your own identity for him. You may think there's something familiar about the man – perhaps he's a bit like someone you think you've met before. Or talked to yourself.

Or perhaps not.

Suffice it to say, stories he told – and stories about him – have been around for thousands of years now.

And if you read between the lines they still make you wonder.

Swap it!

18. Experiment . . .

Here we go, one last time . . .

1. Give yourself permission to take a few quiet minutes as you are reading this to wander down the road of your mind and round the corner to your own private Swap Shop. Go in through the door right now and 'meet Mr Moore' yourself. Just the two of you. He's longing to meet you.
2. Take time to discuss with him the first things that you want to swap, and think about how you came to choose them to go right now.
3. Imagine having what you want to lose actually in your hands, and what you want to gain there on the table in front of you.
4. Here comes the swap. Symbolically put what is in your hands down on the table. Push it away from you with both hands.

Then with both hands pick up what you want instead. Be very clear what it is, and what it is like to have it in your hands.
5. Press it against your chest, and let it slip through your skin and into you.
6. Spend a few moments enjoying your new possession.

You can now go and live differently.

For ever.

Now you have read all about life coaching, you can meet Andrew Sercombe in person via his web site: www.powerchange.com or telephone him on 01903 744399. Alternatively, you can write to him direct at Powerchange, Storrington, West Sussex, RH20 3NA.

What Happens When You Do Anything?

ANDREW SERCOMBE

In the time it takes to read this entertaininingly useful book you will know:

- *The deep secrets of how to change the future*
- *What you would like the future to be!*

Powerchange Master Coach and Trainer Andrew Sercombe invites you to:

*Tip-toe into tomorrow
dance with destiny
take the 'con' out of the consequences!*

0 86347 430 6